T0020643

SCORPION VS. TARANTULA

BY THOMAS K. ADAMSON

BELLWETHER MEDIA · MINNEAPOLIS, MN

Torque brims with excitement
perfect for thrill-seekers of all kinds.
Discover daring survival skills, explore
uncharted worlds, and marvel at mighty
engines and extreme sports. In *Torque* books,
anything can happen. Are you ready?

This edition first published in 2021 by Bellwether Media, Inc.

No part of this publication may be reproduced in whole or in part without written
permission of the publisher. For information regarding permission, write to
Bellwether Media, Inc., Attention: Permissions Department,
6012 Blue Circle Drive, Minnetonka, MN 55343.

Library of Congress Cataloging-in-Publication Data

Names: Adamson, Thomas K., 1970- author.
Title: Scorpion vs. tarantula / by Thomas K. Adamson.
Other titles: Scorpion versus tarantula
Description: Minneapolis, MN : Bellwether Media, 2021. | Series: Torque:
   animal battles | Includes bibliographical references and index. |
   Audience: Ages 7-12 | Audience: Grades 4-6 | Summary: "Amazing
   photography accompanies engaging information about the fighting
   abilities of scorpions and tarantulas. The combination of high-interest
   subject matter and light text is intended for students in grades 3
   through 7"– Provided by publisher.
Identifiers: LCCN 2020041122 (print) | LCCN 2020041123 (ebook) | ISBN
   9781644874622 (library binding) | ISBN 9781648342554 (paperback) |
   ISBN 9781648341397 (ebook)
Subjects: LCSH: Scorpions–Juvenile literature. | Tarantulas–Juvenile literature.
Classification: LCC QL458.7 .A33 2021 (print) | LCC QL458.7 (ebook) | DDC
   595.4/6–dc23
LC record available at https://lccn.loc.gov/2020041122
LC ebook record available at https://lccn.loc.gov/2020041123

Text copyright © 2021 by Bellwether Media, Inc. TORQUE and associated logos
are trademarks and/or registered trademarks of Bellwether Media, Inc.

Editor: Kieran Downs   Designer: Josh Brink

Printed in the United States of America, North Mankato, MN.

TABLE OF CONTENTS

THE COMPETITORS

Some small animals are built for battle! Scorpions are creatures made for fighting. Their large **pincers** and sharp stingers make them battle ready.

Tarantulas are also ready to fight. Their quick speed and deadly **venom** can take down almost any enemy. Who would win in a battle between these two feared **arachnids**?

There are almost 2,000 different **species** of scorpion. Most are about 2.5 inches (6.4 centimeters) long. All scorpions have a hard **exoskeleton**. Their tails curve to a sharp point.

These arachnids can live in **rain forests**, grasslands, and deserts. Some live in cold areas, such as mountains. They hide under rocks and logs most of the time.

EMPEROR SCORPION

SINGING SCORPIONS

Some scorpion species rub their legs together to "sing," much like crickets do.

EMPEROR SCORPION PROFILE

```
|----|----|----|----|----|----|----|----|----|
0         2         4         6         8
INCHES    INCHES    INCHES    INCHES    INCHES
```

HABITAT

RAIN FORESTS

LENGTH

UP TO 7.9 INCHES
(20 CENTIMETERES)

WEIGHT

UP TO 1 OUNCE
(28 GRAMS)

EMPEROR SCORPION RANGE

■ RANGE

MEXICAN RED-KNEE TARANTULA PROFILE

WEIGHT
UP TO 0.5 OUNCES
(14 GRAMS)

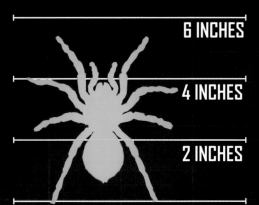

6 INCHES

4 INCHES

LENGTH
UP TO 5.5 INCHES
(14 CENTIMETERS)

2 INCHES

HABITAT

SCRUBLANDS

DESERTS

FORESTS

MEXICAN RED-KNEE TARANTULA RANGE

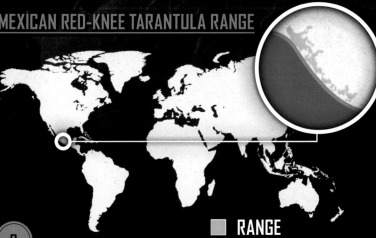

■ RANGE

There more than 800 species of tarantula. They live mostly in warm areas such as deserts and the **tropics**. Including their legs, these hairy spiders can be up to 11 inches (28 centimeters) across.

Tarantulas do not have good eyesight. The hairs on their legs and bodies can sense **vibrations**. This lets tarantulas know what is around them.

MEXICAN RED-KNEE TARANTULA

SECRET WEAPONS

Scorpions sense movement with hairs on their bodies, too. This tells them where their **prey** is. The hairs can feel insect wings flapping in the air.

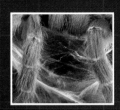
SILK LINES

LONG FANGS

BARBED HAIRS

Some tarantulas set traps. They spin lines of silk at the entrance to their **burrows**. When something touches the silk, tarantulas sense the vibrations. Then they know prey is near.

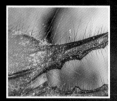

SENSITIVE HAIRS

STRONG PINCERS

VENOMOUS STINGER

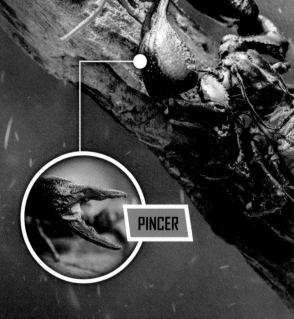

PINCER

Scorpions use their strong pincers to grab prey. They may crush their prey with their pincers. Other times they hold prey down.

0   **1 INCHES**   **2 INCHES**

GOLIATH BIRDEATER FANG
1.5 INCHES (3.8 CENTIMETERS)

GOLIATH BIRDEATER

Tarantulas have two long **fangs**. They use them to bite their prey. Venom from the fangs can kill prey. Tarantulas also have strong jaws to crush prey.

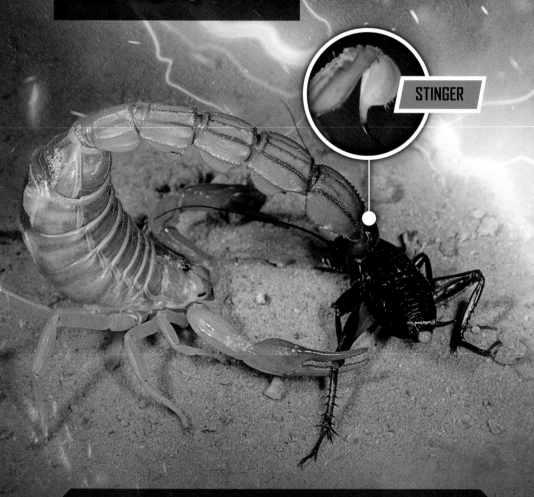

STING STRENGTH

Only about 40 scorpion species have venom strong enough to kill a person. For others, the sting is similar to a bee sting.

STINGER

Scorpions have venomous stingers on their tails. Their stings will stun or kill prey. Scorpions only sting if they have to. Making venom takes energy.

Tarantula hairs are **barbed** at the end.
The spiders use these hairs as **defense**. They flick
them out at attackers. The sharp hairs can stick in
the eyes of enemies.

ATTACK MOVES

When prey is within reach, scorpions quickly rush forward. They grab prey with their large pincers. Not much can escape their grip.

PEDIPALPS

Tarantulas wait for their food. They **ambush** prey when it is close enough. Tarantulas grab onto prey with **pedipalps**. These look like two small legs.

Scorpion tails come down quickly for a sting. The prey cannot move. Scorpions tear it up into little pieces.

STING SPEED

51 INCHES (130 CENTIMETERS) PER SECOND

DEATHSTALKER SCORPION

26 INCHES (66 CENTIMETERS) PER SECOND

SPITTING SCORPION

Tarantulas bite prey with their fangs. Tarantula venom melts prey. The prey turns into a liquid that the spiders can suck into their mouths.

READY, FIGHT!

A tarantula senses movement nearby. A scorpion is out looking for food. The scorpion runs forward to attack. The spider flicks hairs at it. But they only bounce off of the scorpion's exoskeleton.

The scorpion grabs the tarantula with its large pincers. It quickly stings the spider. Soon the spider cannot move. The tarantula was no match for the scorpion's weapons!

GLOSSARY

ambush—to carry out a surprise attack

arachnids—creatures with two body segments and four pairs of legs

barbed—having a sharp point that sticks out and backward from a larger point

burrows—tunnels or holes in the ground used as animal homes

defense—a way to protect

exoskeleton—a hard outer covering on some animals

fangs—long, pointed teeth

pedipalps—small limbs used for grasping or feeling

pincers—curved claws with two sides used to grip things

prey—animals that are hunted by other animals for food

rain forests—thick, green forests that receive a lot of rain

species—kinds of animals

tropics—a hot, rainy region near the equator

venom—a poison produced by some animals

vibrations—very rapid back and forth movements